A New True Book

WATER POLLUTION

By Darlene R. Stille

CHILDRENS PRESS ®
CHICAGO

Polluted water in the Ohio River

PHOTO CREDITS

AP/Wide World Photos—17 (right), 40 (right)

The Bettmann Archive, Inc.—26

© Jerry Hennen—4 (bottom left), 8 (top right), 10 (bottom left), 18 (left), 29 (left)

© Norma Morrison—12 (right), 13 (top right)

Reuters/Bettmann Newsphotos—18 (right)

Shostal Associates/SuperStock International, Inc.—2, 6 (left), 44 (left); © A. T. Hennek, 38

Tom Stack & Associates—© Thomas Kitchin, 4 (top left), 13 (bottom right), 22 (right), 31 (inset); © Larry Lipsky, 8 (left); © Tom Stack, 9 (right), 16; © Dick George, 10 (top right); © Gene Marshall, 13 (left); © Kevin Schafer, 17 (left); © Gary Milburn, 22 (left), 31 (left); © Ken W. Davis, 40 (left); © Kevin Schafer, 44 (right); © Spencer Swanger, 45 (right)

SuperStock International, Inc.—© Manley Photo-Tuscon, Ariz., 14

Valan—© J. Alan Wilkinson, Cover, 29 (right), 33; © Eastcott/Momatiuk, 4 (top right); © Martin Kuhnigk, 4 (bottom right); © Stephen J. Krasemann, 6 (right), 7 (right), 10 (bottom center & bottom right); © Thomas Kitchin, 7 (left), 21 (left); © Tom W. Parkin, 8 (bottom right); © Harold V. Green, 9 (left); © Kennon Cooke, 12 (left); © Jean Bruneau, 21 (right); © Gilles Delisle, 24 (2 photos); © Halle Flygare, 30; © Gilbert van Ryckevorsel, 35, 37; © K. Ghani, 40 (center); © Denis Roy, 42 (left); © Val Wilkinson, 42 (right); © Francis Lepine, 45 (left)

Cover — Pollution in River

Library of Congress Cataloging-in-Publication Data

Stille, Darlene R.
    Water pollution / by Darlene R. Stille.
        p.   cm. — (A New true book)
    Includes index.
    Summary: Discusses the benefits of water, its pollution, and the harmful effects of and ways of avoiding water pollution.
    ISBN 0-516-01190-1
    1. Water—Pollution—Economic aspects—Juvenile literature. [1. Water—Pollution. 2. Pollution.] I. Title.
HC79.W32S75   1990   89-25344
363.73′94—dc20   CIP
                                        AC

TABLE OF CONTENTS

Lakes (top left) and ponds (bottom left) are hollows in the ground that fill with water. Sometimes streams flow gently through meadows (top right), and sometimes they splash over rocks to form white-water rapids (bottom right).

A WORLD OF WATER

Sparkling, clean water is beautiful. Rivers, lakes, ponds, marshes, and oceans are all made of water.

All these are bodies of water that we can easily see. But there is also water hidden underground. It is called groundwater. People drill wells to reach this groundwater.

Streams and rivers, ponds and lakes, marshes and

Rivers from New York City (left) to Fairbanks, Alaska
(right), are polluted by the dumping of trash and garbage.

swamps, groundwater, and
even the oceans are all in
danger today because
people dump garbage and
poisonous wastes carelessly.
This careless dumping
causes water pollution.

WATER IS NEEDED FOR ALL LIFE

Wild animals such as the mule deer (left) and the mountain lion (right) drink water from rivers and streams.

Water pollution is a serious problem because nothing could live on earth without water.

Animals and plants that live on land need water in order to stay alive.

Many plants and animals live in water. Fish are the most familiar water animals. But many other types of

7

Fish called grunts (above), the crab (above right), and the jellyfish (right) are animals that live in the ocean.

animals, from starfish and jellyfish to shrimps and crabs, live in water.

Tiny animals and plants— called plankton—also live in water. They are so small that they can be seen only under a microscope.

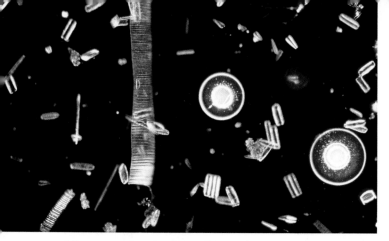

Microscopic plankton (above) are the most easily harmed living thing in water. Animals that eat poisoned plankton can be harmful to humans (right).

If plankton takes up poisonous chemicals polluting the water, the animals that eat plankton also will eat the chemicals. As larger animals eat smaller ones, more poisons will gather in the larger animals. People who eat these animals may be poisoned.

SALT WATER AND FRESH WATER

Some plants and animals live in fresh water and others live in salt water. These are the two basic types of water in the world.

This system of pipes brings fresh groundwater to crops for irrigation.

The green frog (left) lives in freshwater ponds and marshes. The sea otter (center) and bottle-nosed dolphins (right) live in salt water.

Ocean water contains a large amount of salt.

Fresh water has very little salt. Fresh water is found in lakes, ponds, rivers, and streams. Groundwater is fresh water too.

Plants and animals that live in fresh water die if salt water enters their area. People cannot use salt water for drinking. And most plants and animals that live in salt water die if they are placed in fresh water.

A drink of water is refreshing on a hot day, and so is a swim in a pool.

HOW PEOPLE USE WATER

People use water in many ways. The most important use of water is for drinking. Human beings must drink fresh water to live.

Fresh drinking water can come from lakes, rivers, or streams.

People use creatures that live in water for food. Fish and seafood are good to eat. In some countries, people even eat certain kinds of seaweed, a plant that grows in water.

Farmers need water to grow fruits and vegetables.

Boys in Hong Kong catch a horseshoe crab. If the water is polluted, eating the crab could be dangerous.

When crops do not get enough rain, farmers use irrigation systems.

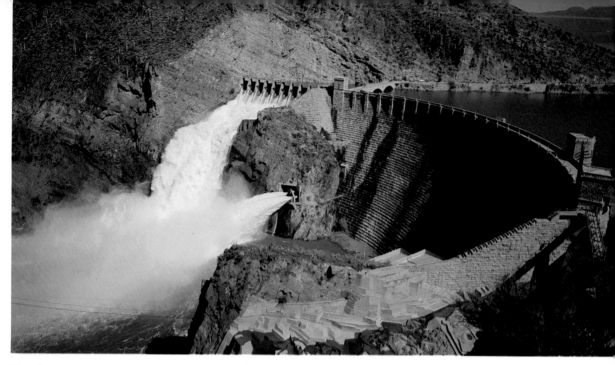

The force of water rushing over Roosevelt Dam in Arizona turns huge wheels connected to turbines that generate electrical power.

Engineers use the power of water to do work.

Water also is used in factories to help make things. It is often mixed with chemicals to make products that range from window cleaner to soda pop.

But some of the ways in which people use water lead to water pollution. Sometimes poisonous chemicals are dumped into the ocean, lakes, or rivers.

Polluted water can harm crops. It can harm plants and animals that live in water. It can harm people who eat these plants and animals and people who drink polluted water.

THINGS THAT POLLUTE WATER

Water polluted by algae

Many different things cause water pollution. Although most water pollution is caused by human beings, some pollution is caused by nature.

Certain types of plants called blue-green algae can poison freshwater ponds. These algae kill the fish in the ponds and the animals that drink the water.

In the ocean, poisons from another type of algae create what scientists call a red tide. A red tide is a rapid growth of algae that gives a reddish color to the water. Some red tides are poisonous to many sea animals.

A red tide (left) off the coast of Mexico. Workers (right) clean up fish killed by a red tide off the coast of St. Petersburg, Florida.

Spirit Lake (above) was polluted by volcanic
ash after Mount St. Helens erupted in 1980.
A child (right) eats beside an open sewer that
carries raw sewage into Hong Kong harbor.

Dust and ash from
erupting volcanoes can
pollute rivers and lakes.
They can turn the river
waters into a thick mud so
that no fish can breathe and
no land animals can drink.
Germs also can pollute

water. Usually this type of pollution is caused by people pouring wastewater from bathrooms directly into rivers or lakes. This kind of wastewater is called sewage.

Salt water can pollute fresh water. This happens in places near the sea. If people drill too many wells to get water for their houses and farms, the seawater may begin to seep into the ground. This salt water can pollute the groundwater.

Heat can pollute water. Heat pollution usually comes from hot water dumped by factories or nuclear power plants. When the heated water is dumped into rivers or lakes, it kills plants and animals.

But most water pollution today is caused by chemicals. These chemicals come from factories or from fertilizers that are used to help crops grow. Oil is another chemical pollutant.

Chemical pollution in marshes (left) affects the food supply of birds and other animals that live there. Waterways in cities (right) can become polluted by chemicals from factories.

Some of the chemicals that pollute water come from garbage dumps. Rainwater may carry chemicals down through the soil and into the groundwater.

Almost 200 chemicals that might be dangerous to our health can be found in drinking water today.

Chemicals in smoke from power plants or factories that burn soft coal cause a

Chemicals in the smoke from factories combine with water in clouds to produce acid rain.

type of water pollution
called acid rain. The smoke
travels high up in the air,
where it mixes with water
in clouds to form an acid.
The acid is milder than lemon
juice, which is also an acid.
But when it falls in rain or
snow on lakes, it makes the
lake water acidic. If the lake
water becomes too acidic,
all the plants and fish die.

A scientist collects water samples (left). In the laboratory (right),
the samples are tested for the presence of chemicals from acid rain.

Not all polluted water
looks dirty. A lake killed by
acid rain looks beautiful
and clean. Its water is very
clear. This is because no
plants or animals live there.

POLLUTION THEN AND NOW

Water pollution has been a problem for thousands of years.

Cities and towns were often built on a lake or river. These lakes or rivers, along with groundwater, provided drinking water for the residents.

But the people dumped their sewage into the same lakes and rivers that provided their drinking water. The wastes filled the

25

A cartoon of the 1800s presents the water of the River Thames in England as "monster soup." Sewage and garbage from the city of London was dumped in the river, making it one of the most polluted waterways in the world.

water with germs. Germs made the people sick. Sometimes there were outbreaks of disease, and many people died.

Chemical wastes from factories also began to

pollute lakes and rivers more than 100 years ago. The factories were often built on waterfronts so that leftover chemicals could be easily dumped in the water.

Chemical pollution of water by lead occurred at least 2,000 years ago. The ancient Romans used lead pipes to carry water from nearby lakes and streams.

Lead is a metal that is very poisonous. Lead harms blood cells, the brain, the nerves, liver, and kidneys. It causes headaches and stomach cramps. Serious lead poisoning can even cause death.

The water that flowed through the lead pipes became polluted. Many Romans suffered from lead poisoning.

Today we know water pipes should not be made of lead. They should be made of copper or plastic.

Today, clean-water laws forbid dumping sewage and poisonous chemicals

Chemicals cause water pollution at a landfill in Illinois
(left) and near a pumping station in Canada (right).

directly into lakes and
streams. But harmful
chemicals still enter our
water. Some chemicals leak
into the water supply with
wastewater from sewers.
Others are spilled accidentally
or dumped illegally.

Because river waters are always flowing, pollutants may be carried into lakes or marshes, or out to sea.

WHAT HAPPENS TO POLLUTED RIVERS

As the river waters flow through the land, they pick up many things, including pollutants.

Because a river may be many miles long, usually only parts of a river become polluted. The polluted area is downstream from the spot where the chemicals or

FRASER RIVER
UNSAFE
FOR BATHING
THE CORP. OF THE TOWNSHIP
OF RICHMOND

Flowing rivers pick up chemicals spilled by factories
and sewage dumped by cities that they pass.

sewage were dumped. So
one section of a river can be
polluted while another
section is clean.

Because river water is
always flowing, a river
can cleanse itself of some

31

kinds of pollution. If no more chemicals or sewage are dumped, the polluted section of the river usually recovers.

How long it takes river water to become clean again depends on how much waste was dumped. Sometimes poisonous chemicals settle into the mud and sand in the riverbed. The chemicals can remain there for years, seeping into the water and killing most of the plants and animals in that section of the river.

WHAT HAPPENS
TO POLLUTED LAKES

Any lake, large or small,
can become polluted. Fish
in some polluted lakes have
poisonous chemicals in their
bodies. Some of these fish
are no longer safe to eat.

Chemical pollutants in the water can kill
thousands of fish in lakes and rivers.

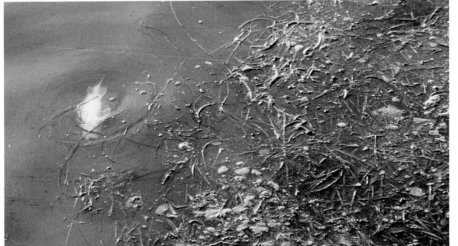

Chemicals and sewage can pollute lakes by making the water unfit for drinking, swimming, or washing. But the greatest problem pollutants create in lakes is the growth of too many plants.

Pollution throws the lake water out of its natural balance. When the water is out of balance, there is too much food for plants and too little oxygen for animals.

When water plants and

The heavy growth of algae in this stream is a sign of pollution.

animals die, they decay and
use up oxygen.

Sewage and other wastes
dumped into a lake also
decay. This makes the waste
harmless, but it uses up
oxygen. Anything that
decays uses up oxygen.

When dead plants and animals and sewage decay, what remains can be used as food by plants. Chemical fertilizers and certain detergents dumped into lakes also provide food for plants.

When there is too much food for plants, too many plants—usually algae—grow in the lake.

Then a strange thing happens. Because there are more plants in the lake, there are more plants to die.

When these plants decay, they use up oxygen that fish and other animals need to breathe.

When the plants decay, they use up huge amounts of oxygen.

Some lakes have so many dead plants decaying that there is very little oxygen left over for the fish.

Sometimes no fish at all

A green-algae "scum" spreads over the surface of a polluted lake in Minnesota. Polluted lakes can be saved by preventing chemical fertilizers, detergents, and sewage from entering the water.

can live there because any oxygen entering the water is immediately used up by the decaying plants.

The natural balance of plants, animals, and oxygen is spoiled. In time, the lake is destroyed.

HOW POLLUTION AFFECTS THE OCEAN

Certain types of pollution can damage the ocean, especially along coastlines.

Oil spills can damage the ocean. Oil floats on the water, causing an oil slick. An oil slick can be carried for great distances by ocean currents. The longer the oil stays in the water, the stickier the oil becomes. Sometimes it forms greasy tar balls.

Left: Workers use a floating barrier called a boom to contain an oil spill. Animals are killed by oil spills. Sticky oil coats the feathers of birds so that they cannot fly (center). It coats the fur of sea mammals so that in cold weather they freeze (right).

Sometimes it washes ashore, coating rocks and sand with black gunk. Wherever the oil slick goes, it kills animals. The

chemicals in the oil poison
sea creatures.

Garbage and chemicals
dumped in the ocean can
also harm life. In shallow
parts of the sea, these
pollutants settle to the
bottom and kill or poison
lobsters, shrimp, and
shellfish. The garbage may
wash up on beaches,
spreading disease-causing
germs.

Pollutants can build up in
the plankton that floats on
the ocean surface. Polluted

Although the ocean is huge, covering more than 70 per cent of the earth, its water is in danger from pollution.

plankton poisons fish and may even poison people who eat the fish.

The ocean is huge and able to cleanse itself of many pollutants. But no one knows how much is too much. That is why scientists believe that nothing harmful should be dumped in the sea.

PROTECTING OUR WATER

Water pollution can be prevented by stronger laws that forbid dumping poisonous chemicals, fertilizers, detergents, and sewage into the lakes, rivers, and oceans.

Sewage can go through special treatment plants that kill germs.

Drinking water can be treated with a chemical called chlorine to kill germs.

Scientists can test drinking

Drinking water is treated in a water plant (left) to make it safe.
The water reclamation plant (right) removes pollution before the
water is released into rivers and streams.

water to be sure it is free of
germs and harmful chemicals.

Water that has been
polluted can be cleaned.
Chemicals can be vacuumed
off the bottom with big hoses.
But this is very expensive.

Scientists are trying to
develop bacteria that will
break down the oil and
make it harmless.

Most water pollution can be prevented by strict laws that forbid dumping pollutants into lakes, rivers, and the ocean, and by constant testing to make sure the water stays clean.

Lakes can be protected from acid rain by making factories and power plants burn hard coal or clean the smoke from furnaces that burn soft coal.

Because water is so important to all life on earth, it must be protected from pollution.

WORDS YOU SHOULD KNOW

acid rain(AS • ihd RAYN)—rainwater that has a high acid content

algae(AL • jay)—tiny plants that live in water

bacteria(back • TEER • ee • ya)—tiny living things that have only one cell and that can be seen only with a microscope

chemicals(KEM • ih • kulz)—materials used in fertilizers and in many manufacturing processes; chemicals are often harmful to living things

chlorine(klor • EEN)—a chemical that is put in water to kill bacteria

decay(dih • KAY)—the process of rotting or breaking down by the action of bacteria

detergents(dih • TER • jints)—soaplike substances, some of which contain phosphates that contribute to the overgrowth of plants in lakes and streams

downstream(down • STREEM)—in the direction toward which the river is flowing

fertilizers(FER • tih • lye • zerz)—materials that contain nutrients to help plants grow

fresh water(FREHSH WAW • ter)—water that has very little salt content

germs(JERMZ)—harmful bacteria that cause diseases

gills(GILZ)—slits at the sides of a fish's head, used for breathing

groundwater(GROUND • waw • ter)—water that has soaked into the ground and is found in pools called aquifers

hard coal(HARD KOLE)—coal that is low in sulfur, a substance that can cause air pollution when the coal is burned

heat pollution(HEET puh • LOO • shun)—the raising of the temperature of a body of water above the normal temperature, so that plants and animals cannot survive

lead poisoning(LED POY • zun • ing) — a diseased condition that occurs when people take the metal lead into their bodies

marsh(MARSH) — low land that is covered with shallow water

microscope(MY • kruh • skohp) — an instrument that makes small objects look larger

nuclear reactor(NOO • clee • er re • ACK • ter) — a machine that releases atomic energy from radioactive materials in a controlled way

oil slick(OYL SLIHK) — a film of oil that floats on top of water after oil has been spilled

oxygen(AHX • ih • jin) — a gas that is found in the air and that humans and animals need to breathe

plankton(PLANK • tun) — tiny plants and animals that live in the ocean

pollutants(puh • LOO • tints) — materials that make air or water unclean

red tide(REHD TYD) — a heavy growth of a certain type of algae that is poisonous to many animals in the water

salt water(SAWLT WAW • ter) — water that contains much salt; ocean water

seaweeds(SEE • weedz) — plants that grow in water

sewage(SOO • idj) — wastewater from homes and factories

soft coal(SAWFT KOLE) — coal that is high in sulfur, an element that can cause air pollution when the coal is burned

well(WEHL) — a hole drilled in the ground, through which groundwater is brought to the surface

INDEX

About the Author

Darlene Stille is a Chicago-based science writer and editor.